52 Weeks of Gratitude

52 positive words that can change your life & the way you think

journal & coloring book
by Kathy Strauss

For more information please contact:
ImageWerks | photography & art
1016 Great Lakes Circle
Myrtle Beach, SC 29588
info@imagewerks.net
Images © 2019 by Kathy Strauss

Printed in the United States of America
10 9 8 7 6 5 4 3 2 1 2017
First printing, 2019

Illustrations and book design by
Kathy Strauss, ImageWerks

Kathy Strauss offers a wide range of services through ImageWerks lc:
- Photography services
- Creative coaching
- Workshops, retreats, and classes
- Commissioned artwork
- Presentations/teambuilding

For information, contact
ImageWerks
1016 Great Lakes Circle
Myrtle Beach, SC 29588
info@imagewerks.net
kathy@imagewerks.net

Additional copies of *52 Weeks of Gratitude* may be ordered through ImageWerks or online.

To order, please contact ImageWerks or visit: www.imagewerks.net.

This book is dedicated to my husband, GC... for all his support and encouragement on this crazy path called life. And to my Mom & Dad, for always knowing that I would follow my artistic vision.

52 Weeks of Gratitude!!

I created & published my first coloring book in 2017 (Coloring Your Spirit: Designs & Meditations to Spark the Creative in All of Us). It was a vision that I had in my "minds eye" for years—but I never did anything with it. It wasn't until I got a small little push from a friend who had seen me doodling during a board meeting & told me that I should create a coloring book. Ever since that meeting, to the time I hit "publish" on my book—I've been creating new pieces that I know will be a series.

All my life I have been doodling some sort of drawing. I've always been in the creative world—but never really did anything that was "for me". Yes, I spent most of my career as a graphic designer and now a professional photographer—but, I have to admit that I am most at peace when I am doing my fine art photography and yes, my doodles. As the years past, I finally got the courage to pick up a paintbrush again to create paintings that I consider good enough to put in the gallery where I show my work. That being said, I my camera is my go to creating tool and of course—my doodles.

So why a journal/coloring book on gratitude? I've been studying with several coaches and it always comes back to the philosophy—that the more you hold gratitude in the forefront of your mind, the easier it becomes to create positive things in your life. I love encouraging people to do their best—as my friends, family members & clients know, I can be their biggest cheerleader. They will tell you too that it's not just them I cheer on—it's anyone that comes into my sphere. My why for being that "cheerleader". . . I do it because I know that each person has a spark of good in each of us. I encourage each of you to tap into that good, once we do—say "thank-you" & with each thank you we say, it will become a tidal wave of gratitude that washes over everything we touch & do in our life.

This journal is set up as a coloring book and a weekly journal. 52 weeks—52 positive words of encouragement. These words are there for you to help spark a conversation that you can use as your theme for the week. The doodle is based on one of my favorite flowers—the sunflower. It is holds a symbolic meaning of faith, longevity, healing, focus, long life, good luck, focus, magic, vitality, intelligence, spiritual knowing and happiness. I chose drawing it to help ground the journaling pages as you write each week what you are grateful for.

The world is in a constant state of creation, and we are responsible for the world we create. We are the artists of our lives... together each of our thoughts, words and actions create a world that is better, colorful, and more beautiful each & every day.

May you gain more peace as you meditate on each of the words & of course then color and journal each week. My wish is that you become conscious and intentional in actions—both individually, collectively, and creatively.

—grateful creative blessings, Kathy

Words of gratitude are a celebration of recognition. You can recognize a specific person, you can recognize yourself or you can simply recognize life as amazing as it is.

It goes much deeper than the words "Thank" & "You." When we hold gratitude in the forefront of our thoughts, everyday events in our life become miraculous. By understanding & expressing gratitude, we increase the flow of good into our life. Look at the word that is for each week, meditate on that word. Then journal & color where you find the gratitude within them. As you do this, watch with amazement as your emotions shift and the ordinary becomes astounding.

Gratitude & focusing on the blessings you already have, is the best affirmation out there.

Abundant

I am so happy & grateful for...

Appreciation

I am so happy & grateful for...

Artist

I am so happy & grateful for...

Week 4

Beautiful

I am so happy & grateful for...

Week 5

Believe

I am so happy & grateful for...

Blessed

I am so happy & grateful for...

Breathe

I am so happy & grateful for...

Week 8

Calm

I am so happy & grateful for...

Celebrate

I am so happy & grateful for...

Week 10

Charitable

I am so happy & grateful for...

Cherish

I am so happy & grateful for...

Clarity

I am so happy & grateful for...

Week 13

Compassion
I am so happy & grateful for...

Week 14

Confident

I am so happy & grateful for...

Week 15

Creative

I am so happy & grateful for...

Embrace

I am so happy & grateful for...

Emotion

I am so happy & grateful for...

Encourage

I am so happy & grateful for...

Energy

I am so happy & grateful for...

Explore

I am so happy & grateful for...

Week 21

Faith

I am so happy & grateful for...

Week 22

Family

I am so happy & grateful for...

Freedom

I am so happy & grateful for...

Friendship

I am so happy & grateful for...

Week 25

Generous

I am so happy & grateful for...

Week 26

Genuine

I am so happy & grateful for...

Week 27

Grace

I am so happy & grateful for...

Week 28

Happy

I am so happy & grateful for...

Harmony

I am so happy & grateful for...

Week 30

Healthy

I am so happy & grateful for...

Week 31

Honest

I am so happy & grateful for...

Hug

I am so happy & grateful for...

Imagination

I am so happy & grateful for...

Inspire

I am so happy & grateful for...

Intuitive
I am so happy & grateful for...

Kindness

I am so happy & grateful for...

Leadership

I am so happy & grateful for...

Love

I am so happy & grateful for...

Week 39

Motivate

I am so happy & grateful for...

Peace
I am so happy & grateful for...

Week 41

Resilience

I am so happy & grateful for...

Smile

I am so happy & grateful for...

Soul

I am so happy & grateful for...

Week 44

Spirit

I am so happy & grateful for...

Week 45

Success

I am so happy & grateful for...

Week 46

Support

I am so happy & grateful for...

Thankful

I am so happy & grateful for...

Week 48

Trust

I am so happy & grateful for...

Week 49

Value

I am so happy & grateful for...

Week 50

Victory

I am so happy & grateful for...

Welcome

I am so happy & grateful for...

Week 52

Yes
I am so happy & grateful for...

About the illustrator/author

Kathy Strauss, CCFC

Website: www.imagewerks.net
facebook: imagewrks
twitter: imagewrk
Pinterest: imagewerks
Instagram: imagewerks

Background: With a background in design and a certification as a Creatively FitTM Coach, Kathy has been in the creative industry for over 40 years. She found her creative voice with her camera and uses it to tell stories for personal branding, commercial clients & families. Fine art is her "release", using her camera to show the world how she sees it & her mixed media work – a tapping into the universal energy that surrounds us. She was a founding artist at the Workhouse Arts Center and President of the Arches Gallery Artists in Lorton, VA prior to moving to Myrtle Beach, SC. She is a published coloring book author, you can find her books on Amazon. She is passionate about the arts and contributing to the community that she now calls home.

Influences: Everything that surrounds us on a daily basis influences Kathy's artwork. The camera is an extension of how Kathy sees the world. She aims to connect her images to the viewer—showing a right brainer's view of the world. From a simple blade of grass, a stark looking building, creating a visual personal brand for a person or company—to the laughing smiles of a family— she captures beauty with her lens. Her personal/creative philosophy is, "I know my job is done when my client looks at their photos & they see their story". As a mixed media artist, she creates her pieces by tapping into the energy that surrounds us. Whether it's a painting of a beloved pet or creating a doodle for one of her coloring books—she creates with the flow. As a Creatively FitTM Coach she shares her artist's view of life through workshops where her students learn how to tap into their innate creativity & enthusiasm for life.

Artistic philosophy & statement: "Live life, love life, paint life, create life! I love showing people that as humans, we are innately creative & everyone's an artist. I love sharing my passion of creativity, taking pictures, telling stories, and giving back. I'm an artist, photographer... I am a visual storyteller".

Have you ever walked by a scene & what you see takes your breath away? You remember these images in your dreams, they might be clear, they might be small & slightly out of focus... but for some reason it sticks with you... you feel it's energy... it makes you feel good. I try to capture this energy in each piece I create—allowing the viewer to feel.

My design background actually comes to life in my artwork. I compose my photographs with precision and harmony—sensitive to graphic composition, repetition, color, rhythm, reflection, pattern and aesthetics— always look at what makes the scene spark. My doodle art comes from my heart—I never know where the piece is going to take me, I allow it to vibrate as I create it and when it's finished, it always amazes me. I enjoy seeing how my heART connects to the piece. But, no matter what I shoot or create, I always see the balance and composition between the elements.

. . . Is it the graphic design influence . . . or a natural appeal for composition? . . .

Made in the USA
Lexington, KY
02 November 2019